*Catechesis*

THE AGHA SHAHID ALI PRIZE IN POETRY

# CATECHESIS

*a postpastoral*

*Lindsay Lusby*

*With a foreword by* KIMIKO HAHN

THE UNIVERSITY OF UTAH PRESS

*Salt Lake City*

AGHA SHAHID ALI

PRIZE IN POETRY

THE AGHA SHAHID ALI PRIZE IN POETRY
*Series Editor:* Katharine Coles
*Advisory Editor:* Paisley Rekdal

The Defiance House Man colophon is a registered trademark of The University of Utah Press. It is based on a four-foot-tall Ancient Puebloan pictograph (late PIII) near Glen Canyon, Utah.

LIBRARY OF CONGRESS CATALOGING-IN-PUBLICATION DATA
Names: Lusby, Lindsay, author. | Hahn, Kimiko, 1955- writer of foreword.
Title: Catechesis : a postpastoral / Lindsay Lusby ; with a foreword by
 Kimiko Hahn. Description: Salt Lake City : The University of Utah Press,
[2019] | Series: The Agha Shahid Ali prize in poetry | Identifiers: LCCN
2018051872 (print) | LCCN 2018053080 (ebook) | ISBN 9781607816980 () |
ISBN 9781607816973 (pbk. : alk. paper) Subjects:| LCGFT: Poetry.
Classification: LCC PS3612.U778 (ebook) | LCC PS3612.U778 A6 2019
(print) | DDC 811/.6--dc23
LC record available at https://lccn.loc.gov/2018051872

Errata and further information on this and other titles
available at UofUpress.com

Printed and bound in the United States of America.

How odd the girl's life looks
Behind this soft eclipse!

—*Emily Dickinson, "Apocalypse"*

# Contents

# Foreword

Dear reader, do you long for a bit of country breeze and shafts of sun across meadow flowers? sandwiches and wine by a lake? take a break from current events? In today's post-pastoral world, where hurricanes increasingly smash homes and hog-waste floods into reservoirs, *stay put*. Pick up this catechism for a few lessons on how one begins to chase the truth and to survive the apocalypse.

In her debut collection, Lindsay Lusby has worked some sorcery of the aberrant kind one knows from childhood wonder tales. Her strict spell-like lines pulse as one learns that the girl who gave birth to an apple

> *. . . is all milkfever*
> *and honeysuckling:*
>
> *vining uptrunk and arching*
> *over herself back and back.*

In other poems, the clipped near-fragments are less spells than outright taunts:

> *Give chase*
> *and she moves like scattershot*
> *constellates over marsh . . .*

Spells, taunts, grim reportage—all of Lusby's craft is in the service of bringing you, the reader, so close you can smell ~~earth, skin, plants in~~ landscapes we know from dream material and bedtime stories.

Another essential dimension of Lusby's craft is her use of popular culture, popular as in folk tales and the canonical narratives/films *The Silence of the Lambs* and *Alien*. (Dr. Freud, dare I suggest *Papa* and *Mama* respectively?) Not familiar? Please queue them up for viewing but meantime you can just bask in the heady juxtapositions. For instance, a line from the poem titled, "Do you spook easily, Starling?":

> *Every shattered thing underfoot*
> *we will call evidence.*

Evidence, yes. Hers. Mine. Yours. And in reference to the mother in *Alien*:

> *You want to know what it is*
> *to play Mother?*
>
> *A fist furled inside your gut,*
> *tight as a fiddlehead,*
>
> *then the moment it splits*
> *open your abdomen . . .*

And speaking of juxtapositions, accompanying these spare poems are off beat extra-illustrations for the reader's comfort and discomfort, curiosity being what it is. These visuals both interrupt and jam together pictures with bits of text. It's quite startling to make the acquaintance of a sprig of "False Dragonhead," the stem of which is a spinal column; whose blossoms are compared to teeth. (More *evidence?*)

In these pages, I've found some of what has become lost in our still-new millennium: a belief that the anomaly is holy. And I've noted what remains: a father mistakes his daughter for a tree, a *Starling* is questioned about a skin suit, and the newborn is monstrous as the mother. If asked to take heart, in these realms, is no less than an invitation to consume.

So, now that I've made introductions, welcome to a world that is as familiar in its twists and churns, as it is uncommonly new. Lusby, through tales old and popular-cultured, has stitched a Frankenstein's infant for us. You will marvel at this daring and true collection. And if, at end, even your appetite feels treacherous, at least you feel alive enough to hunger.

*Kimiko Hahn*
Salt Lake City, Utah

*Woman of the Apocalypse*

# Girl with no Hands

Her own father mistook her for an apple tree,
full-trunked and red-cheeked.

So he hacked at limbs,
a bedlam of branches and hands.

He believed in the fruits of his delirium:

    that the daughter-tree cut back
    would grow wiser next year,

    that the bees come to roost
    would sweeten the crop.

He tells her:

    *If you love me,*
    *you will leaf and bud.*

    *If you love me,*
    *you will ripen.*

# Interlude

A girl has two choices:

> to be a tree or
> to be the forest.

If she leaves her father's house,
she can shrink into

> the dark alleys between oaks,
> brimming gutters under brush

with so many eyes shining out.

They will coo at her,
call her *red-delicious* or *pink lady*.

If she has no hands,
she will go headfirst:

> by the skin of her teeth,
> by the point of her chin,

sharpening as she runs.

If she follows that beating black bird,
she will tangle herself in understory,

in those quiet degrees of shade.

# Forestry (part one)

The girl with no hands
prefers to imagine herself
a bird:

       pink pigeon feet
       and tiny holey bones—

the heart-in-throat murmurs.


An unhanded bird
               is still a bird,
is still worth its weight in breadcrumbs.

# Forestry (part two)

The girl with no hands
carries her heart in her teeth,

       a muffled two-step
       that becomes her name:

twig-snap and recoil,
soil-deep in bear trap.

       It all hinges on bone
       and ligament—

this lockjaw-love,
its metallic aftertaste.

# Forestry (part three)

The girl with no hands
listens behind her

      for the tramping
          of lumberjacks,

the temper of boots against bark.


If a felled girl falls in a forest,
does it sound

      inevitable?  A flogged
          girl dragged back

to the sawmill.  She hears

      the swarming rattle
          of locusts.

*Lamb of Law*

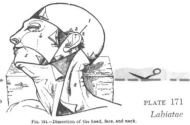

# HOODED SKULLCAP

*Scutellaria epilobiifolia*

PLATE 171

*Labiatae*

FIG. 194.—Dissection of the head, face, and neck.

The numerous species of Skullcap can all be recognized by the peculiar shape of the corolla, which becomes an elongated, curved, ascending tube with a dilated throat. Terminating the tube are two lips, the upper short and either entire or slightly notched, the lower lip spreading and three lobed. These are bitter rather than aromatic plants, they have the Mint family's characteristic opposite leaves and perennial roots. The Hooded Skullcap grows erect, one to three feet in height, with ovate pointed leaves which are often heart-shaped at the base. The flowers, up to an inch in length, growing singly or in small clusters in the upper leaf axils, each corolla has a helmet-shaped upper lip. The usual color is blue violet with a white throat and tube, however, rose-colored and white varieties occur. Hooded Skullcap prefers gravelly or rocky shores and wet meadows for its home, its range is from Newfoundland across to Alaska and from Delaware west to Arizona and California. The flowers first appear in June and continue through September.

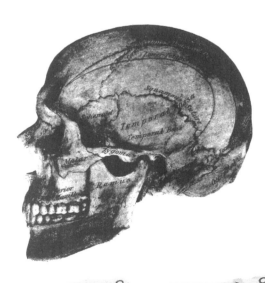

# Do you spook easily, Starling?

A stone slungshot in the brush
        is a body facedown in the river—

we drop our scavenging
                and scatter.

Every shattered thing underfoot
        we will call evidence.

The map we make of it:
            a murder.

bone

boneash

boneblack

bone china

boned

bone-dry

bonefish

bonehead

bone marrow

bonemeal

bone oil

bone saw

boneset

bonesetter

boneyard

Fig. 4. Fig. 5.

F. Frontal Bone; M Mandible; O. Occipital
Bone; S. Suture marking off parietal bone; T.
Squamosal Bone; V. Parietal Bone

PLATE 217

Boneset, *Eupatorium perfoliatum*

## That is rather slippery of you, Agent Starling.

When the truth is small enough
      to fit in your cupped hands,

you chase it with a broom
      to every corner of the house

to pin its bristling body there
      against the papered cabbage roses.


When it beats between your fingers,
      all sinew-snap and barbed air,

you will know it is less hope than feather,
      more crush than bone.

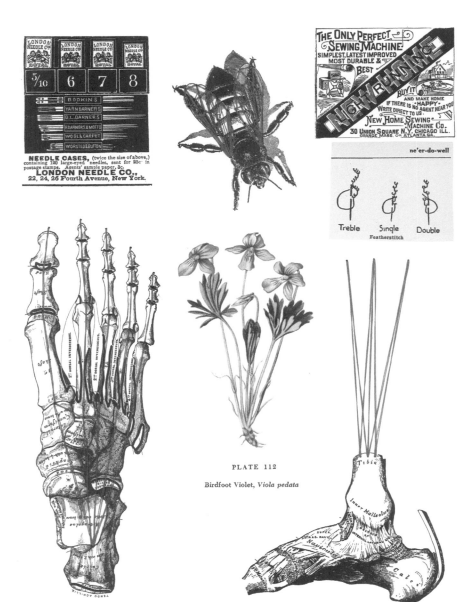

PLATE 112

Birdfoot Violet, *Viola pedata*

Fig. 189.—Ankle-joint: tarsal and tarso-metatarsal articulations. Internal view. Right side.

# Why do you think he removes their skins, Agent Starling?

Are you a bird
      in a woman-suit, Clarice?

Some pretty little blood sparrow—
such lungspan,
             such bright palpitation:

*redthread.   redthread.   redthread.*

Peeled back,
          you are the same shade
of robin-redbreast.

            You are plucked up.

Ready for love
      to wear you like a girl-pelt

          and preen.

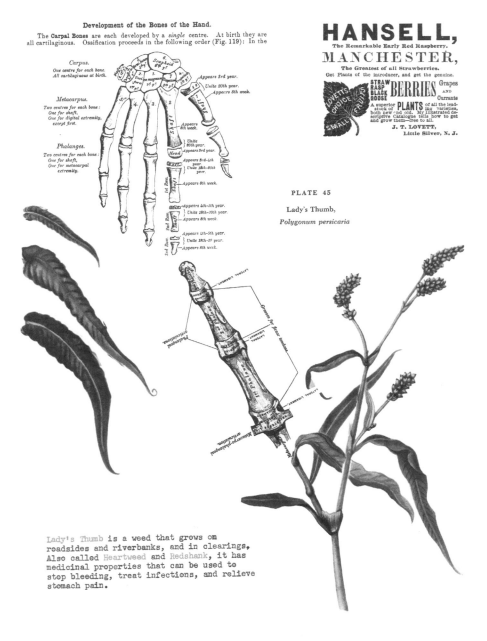

## Development of the Bones of the Hand.

The **Carpal Bones** are each developed by a *single* centre. At birth they are all cartilaginous. Ossification proceeds in the following order (Fig. 119): In the

**Carpus.**
One centre for each bone.
All cartilaginous at birth.

**Metacarpus.**
Two centres for each bone :
One for shaft.
One for digital extremity,
except first.

**Phalanges.**
Two centres for each bone :
One for shaft,
One for metacarpal
extremity.

PLATE 45

Lady's Thumb,
*Polygonum persicaria*

Lady's Thumb is a weed that grows on roadsides and riverbanks, and in clearings. Also called Heartweed and Redshank, it has medicinal properties that can be used to stop bleeding, treat infections, and relieve stomach pain.

# Look at him, Starling. Tell me what you see.

*or, still life with crime scene photos*
*and newspaper clippings*


We will know him by
         the bodies of his work:

an arm unsleeved of skin,
                              and another,

a blouse split up the back
like a ladybird.


Witness in the mudwell of a bootprint:
         gunpowder and mothwing.

                                   There,
a ditchdeep arrangement
                         of ankles.

Here, a headline reads:
*Fathers, Hide Your Daughters.*

PLATE 173

(*left*) Common Nightshade, *Solanum nigrum*

(*right*) Bittersweet, *Solanum dulcamara*

deaths head
hawk moth

1
POUND
PURE
HONEY

"Somebody grew this guy. Fed
him honey & nightshade, kept
him warm. Somebody loved him."

# How do we begin to covet, Clarice?

*after L'Air du Temps, Nina Ricci*

When a look is not enough,
　　you must dig a hole inside her

and bury your ruin there.

　　In the hollow of her,

offerings of clove bud and oakmoss,
　　sawdust and rose-water.

Smell the florid rot of want,

　　the humid musk of need.

Let them choke on each other
　　until they are one blurred retching:

a wintering hawkmoth

　　pulled whole from your throat.

Sheep Laurel is a shrub commonly found
in old-growth fields and pastures. But
it also blooms furiously after fresh
wildfires. Sometimes called Lambkill
because of a poison in its leaves which
causes honey intoxication.

# WILD FLOWERS,
—OF—
## NORTH AMERICA.

☞Our most desirable PERENNIAL PLANTS
for Cultivation.☜
Orchids, Ferns, Lilies, Aquatics, Alpine,
and Sub-Alpine Plants.

Botanical and Common names given.   Send for Cata-
logue.        EDWARD GILLETT, Southwick, Mass.

PLATE 136

Sheep Laurel, *Kalmia angustifolia*

# Have the lambs stopped screaming?

When you find him,
  will you ask

    for a glass of water
    for a handful of sugar

 to use the phone?

    Already,

she is hanging inside him
  from a meathook,

    a field-dressed tenderfoot
    swinging by her ankles.

 Does he know

   that you know?


When he is asleep,
  rip him open

   like a barndoor.

*Woman of the Apocalypse*

# Girl with Cloven Feet

A hunger for green things
starts in the toes,

                    lingers at the hedges
      on deersoft steps.

She waits for nightcover
to track past clover and henbit,

            to garden lettuces and parsley
and strips them down to topsoil.

The hunger for knowings
starts in the fingers,

                plucks every *thou-shalt-not*,

holds each petal on her tongue
like a sacrament:

            *He loves me.*
                  *He loves me not.*

# Trespass

If a hooved girl is caught in headlights,

      she will hold her breath
and imagine impact.

If her ribcage is cleaved open,

      He will cut out her heart,
transplant an apple.

He will call this even.

# Trade

Hers is a false pulsing:

> a lightstruck object
> mocking life like a moon,

and just as thimble-pocked.

> This heart, a salt lick
> in its spring-loaded bone-cage.

# Trigger

The girl with cloven feet
has no shadow left

      to drag behind her
         like fletching,

like a dark and feathered aftermath.

         Call her *Arrowhead*.
Call her *Deerhide without a copse*.

She is a whitetail
      in a fallow field,

         a jacklight gleam
         above the sedge.

# Tremble

The girl with cloven feet
walks home alone at night.

          In the pitch,
       she is all eyeshine:

ghost-stars disturbing the dark,
          drifting deeper into thicket
                    into lost-track.

Give chase
and she moves like scattershot,
        constellates over marsh:

           a smile studded as a belt,
       the flint-strike of tooth on light.

The sink-swell
of this drowning ground,
              a reckoning.

# The Dragon

# ROUND-LEAVED SUNDEW

PLATE 74

*Drosera rotundifolia*                                           *Droseraceae*

The Sundews are a widespread genus of peculiar plants, with more than 80 species scattered throughout the world, seven of them occur in eastern United States. Round-leaved Sundew has a low-growing cluster of flat and rounded leaves with long hairy stems; the leaves seem to cling close to the ground and are often hidden by grasses. Each leaf has a glistening red appearance because of the many red-stalked hairs covering its surface, each hair in reality a gland tipped with mucilage. The resulting glistening effect gives the impression of a dew-covered plant. The leaves, about the size of a small coin, look like little harmless pincushions; but the unwary insect which steps on one is caught by the glandular hairs, eventually dies, and its digestible remains are absorbed by the leaves. Sundew flowers grow in a one-sided terminal cluster. Round-leaved Sundew occurs across the continent from Labrador to Alaska and from Florida to California, wherever there is peaty or moist acid soil. The flowers appear during the summer.

PLATE 74

Venus Flytrap,
*Dionaea muscipula*

Round-leaved Sundew,
*Drosera rotundifolia*

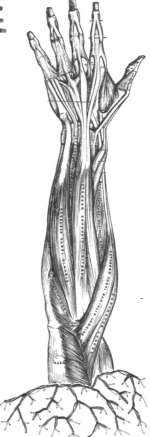

# What's the story, Mother?

Take comfort in this:
you are not dear to me.

O Night of Desirable Objects,
you are the honeytrap
                  I cast deep

into this bracken of asters
and catchflies.
                You will watch

the dark undress,
peel back its beard of sepals.

      Do not call out for me:

Let this pale hand cover your mouth.
Let it smother you with my love.

# JACK-IN-THE-PULPIT

The margins of ponds and swamps, as well as muddy and wet habitats  generally, are also the home of members of the Arum family.

7, spadix with spathe (d).

ARTICULATIONS OF THE

UPPER EXTREMITY.

PLATE 2

Jack-in-the-pulpit, *Arisaema triphyllum*

borne on the fleshy stalk of a spadix.

As in the cat- tails, the flowers are small and inconspicuous,

Wait a minute, there's movement.
It seems to have life—organic life.

*Denver corpse flower finally blooms, stinks up botanic garden.*
—headline from *The Washington Post*, August 19, 2015

You want to know what it is
        to play Mother?

A fist furled inside your gut,
        tight as a fiddlehead,

then the moment it splits
        open your abdomen:

a bloom of umbilicus
        purpling like dead meat,

your own doom pushing up and up
        leaves you a blown-out husk,

still warm, still wet. When they come
        to collect what's left, tell them

it was never worth this.

Right upper.

Lower.

*Flower Structure and*

*Type of Inflorescence*

1st cervical
or Atlas.

2nd cervical
or Axis.

3

4

5

6

7

1

2

3

4

5

6

7

8

9

10

11

12

1st lumbar.

2

3

4

5

Sacrum.

Coccyx.

PLATE 170

False Dragonhead, *Physostegia virginiana*

# You still don't understand
# what you're dealing with, do you?

Inside its mouth,
                    another mouth:

        a fearful symmetry that rips
through every soft-bellied thing

    like worms through wet earth.


On top of bone,
                    more moonbright bone.

        Holds the nightbloom of your face
in thrall and you will tremble at the feet

    of all its terrible glory.


Behold, child:
                    this is Leviathan.

Swamp Pink is a woodland flower also known as Dragon's-mouth.

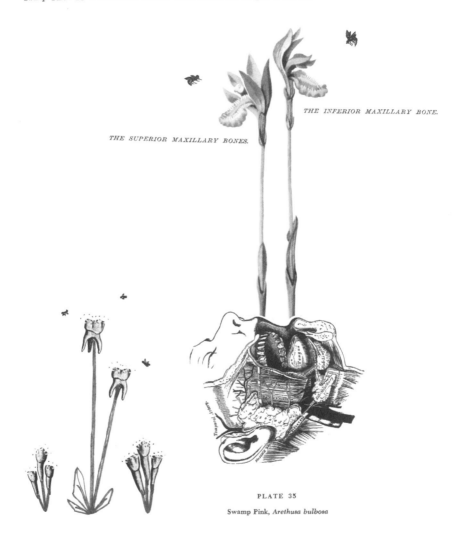

THE SUPERIOR MAXILLARY BONES.

THE INFERIOR MAXILLARY BONE.

PLATE 35

Swamp Pink, *Arethusa bulbosa*

I can't lie to you about your chances,
but you have my sympathies.


The truth is
when you die in your dreams
            you wake here:

sap-stuck beneath a juniper,
bones turning back to eggwhite.

What kind of Mother
watches Her children consumed
            and does not consume Herself?

Your small body held milkwarm
in the throat and unmade there.

Now: *make it new again.*

As above

Scarious Blazing Star, *Liatris scariosa*

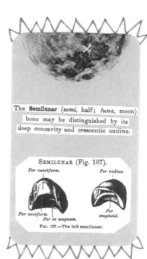

The **Semilunar** (*semi*, half; *luna*, moon) bone may be distinguished by its deep concavity and crescentic outline.

SEMILUNAR (Fig. 107).

For cuneiform.                    For radius.

For unciform.
For os magnum.                    For scaphoid.

FIG. 107.—The left semilunar.

PLATE 227

Blazing Star, *Liatris pycnostachya*

So below

We've got this far—we must go on.
We have to go on.


You come back as a bird
in the air shafts,

strike yourself against
the walls like a match
                    and burn.

Little flamethrower,
your Mother is counting

down the seconds until
She is no one's Mother.

              Mother airlocked,
                    Mother sputtering,

Mother singing her last birdprayer:
    *ashes ashes we all fall down.*

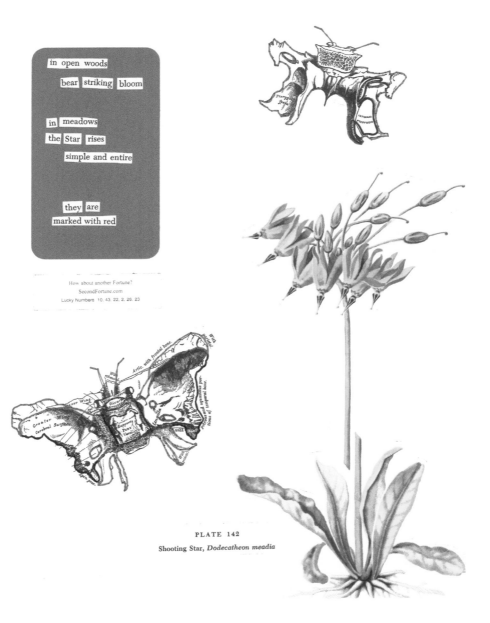

in open woods

bear striking bloom

in meadows
the Star rises
simple and entire

they are
marked with red

PLATE 142

Shooting Star, *Dodecatheon meadia*

# You are my lucky star.

My unmothered bird,

dropped from the sky
    like a millstone.


If you outlive the fall,
crawl from your crater

like the second coming,
    like the swell of new growth

after fire: just briars and briars
and briars.

*Woman of the Apocalypse*

# Girl who Gave Birth to an Apple

Some might call it a miracle:
    this immaculate fruit dropping

from her womb

        like windfall.

She licks it clean: every ounce of
    afterbirth thick and sweet as

spilled honey.

        This kind of nature

considers eating its young:
    a red-handed proof of love.

She weighs it in units

        of hunger,

then swaddles it in apron,
    admires the mottled skin:

how it blushes,

        how it pales.

*Blessed art thou among orchards.*
    *Blessed is the yield of thy branches.*

# Worms

The girl who gave birth to an apple
            cradles the aftermath

      in a sparrow's nest
            and sends it downstream.

She thinks of circling fruit-flies:
            tiny thorns unraveling

      that mealy body, its sweet meat
            like the inside of a beehive.

She thinks of it as a writhing
            thing with no name:

      some still life, interrupted.

# Ditchweed

The girl who gave birth to an apple

is a mother half-full,
                is a girl half-empty.

She is all milkfever
                and honeysuckling:

vining uptrunk and arching
                over herself back and back.

A craving for dandelion
                buds up her throat

and leaves her mouth
                a litany of yellow.

# Roadkill

The girl who gave birth to an apple

      is a bird-broken window,
is a seam snagged open:

cold air balloons her belly
      with the idea of fullness—

the idea of bursting
      at a happy matchstrike.

# Interlude (again)

If a girl lay shoulder-to-shoulder
with the road,
                               she will play dead:
         head slung backwise,
                  tongue hung out like entrails.

If she waits up for the moon,
she will waxen:
                          dew settled in her lungs
         and milkfat in her cheek.

Pinch her:
                  she will mold herself
              around that touch.

# Notes

The poem titles in the "Lamb of Law" series are lines of dialogue borrowed from the film *The Silence of the Lambs* (1991), directed by Jonathan Demme. Quoted text included in *"(nightshade & bittersweet / plate 173)"* is also a line of dialogue borrowed from this film.

The poem titles in "The Dragon" series are lines of dialogue borrowed from *Alien* (1979), directed by Ridley Scott.

The "Girl with No Hands" poem series draws from the Brothers Grimm fairy tale popularly called "The Maiden without Hands."

In "Why do you think he removes their skins, Agent Starling?," the phrase "robin-redbreast" is borrowed from William Blake's poem "Auguries of Innocence."

In "You still don't understand what you're dealing with, do you?," the phrase "fearful symmetry" is borrowed from William Blake's poem "The Tyger."

\*\*\*

The following source texts were used in the making of the "Lamb of Law" & "The Dragon" poem collages. The use of these source materials meets the criteria for determination of fair use, and so falls under its protection:

*The Compleat Farmer: A Compendium of Do-It-Yourself, Tried and True Practices for the Farm, Garden, and Household.* The Main Street Press (1975).

*Gray's Anatomy (1901 Edition)*. Henry Gray, F.R.S. (1974).

*The MacMillan Wild Flower Book*. Clarence Hylander & Edith Farrington Johnston (1954).

*Webster's Unified Dictionary and Encyclopedia*. H.S. Stuttman Company, Inc. (1961).

# Acknowledgments

Grateful acknowledgment is made to the journals and anthologies in which the following poems first appeared.

*The Account: A Journal of Poetry, Prose, and Thought*: "What's the story, Mother?" and "You still don't understand what you're dealing with, do you?"

*bramble & thorn* (Porkbelly Press, 2017): "Trespass" and "Tremble"; "Trade" was reprinted here.

*The Cincinnati Review*: "You are my lucky star."

*Dream Pop Press*: "(lady's thumb / plate 45)" and "(nightshade & bittersweet / plate 173)"

*Duende*: "(hooded skullcap / plate 171)"; "(false dragonhead / plate 170)"; "(jack-in-the-pulpit / plate 2)"; "(round-leaved sundew & venus flytrap / plate 74)"; and "(swamp pink / plate 35)"

*Faerie Magazine*: "Girl with Cloven Feet"; "Trade"; and "Trigger"

*Fairy Tale Review*: "Forestry (part one)"; "Forestry (part two)"; and "Forestry (part three)" as "Forestry (parts 1-3)"

*The Feminist Wire*: "Girl with no Hands" and "Interlude"

*North Dakota Quarterly*: "Do you spook easily, Starling?" and "Interlude (again)"

*Passages North*: "Wait a minute, there's movement. It seems to have life—organic life."

*Still Life with Poem: Contemporary Natures Mortes in Verse* (Literary House Press, 2016): "Look at him, Starling. Tell me what you see." was reprinted here.

*Third Point Press*: "That is rather slippery of you, Agent Starling"; "How do we begin to covet, Clarice?"; and "Have the lambs stopped screaming?"

*Tinderbox Poetry Journal*: "Why do you think he removes their skins, Agent Starling?" and "Look at him, Starling. Tell me what you see."

*The Wolf Skin*: "Girl who Gave Birth to an Apple"

***

The "Girl with no Hands" poem series, "Girl with Cloven Feet" poem series, and "Girl who Gave Birth to an Apple" poem series were all previously published as a chapbook titled *Blackbird Whitetail Redhand* (Porkbelly Press, 2018).

"Forestry (parts 1-3)" won the 2015 *Fairy Tale Review* Poetry Contest, judged by Joyelle McSweeney.

"Wait a minute, there's movement. It seems to have life—organic life." was nominated for *Best New Poets 2018* by *Passages North*.

# Special Thanks

Thank you to Kimiko Hahn for selecting my first book *Catechesis: A postpastoral* for the 2018 Agha Shahid Ali Poetry Prize. I'm grateful to Hannah New and the staff at The University of Utah Press for bringing my book to life.

To my mentors and great friends, Jehanne Dubrow and James Allen Hall: thank you for your encouragement and guidance, your generosity of time and spirit, and the example of your dedication to a life in poetry. Thank you to Emma Sovich, my dearest friend and trusted first reader. I am so grateful to all of the good friends (inside the poetry world and out) who have been so supportive of my work, especially Julie Armstrong, Bryanna Tidmarsh & Michael VanCalbergh, Jenny Gallagher, Michele Santamaria, Eleanor & Caroline Harvey, Julie Marie Wade, Leslie Harrison, Terri Witek, Heidi Czerwiec, Shara Lessley, Sally Rosen Kindred, and Emily Kalwaitis. Thank you to Nicci Mechler and Porkbelly Press for supporting so many of these poems. Thank you to the Rose O'Neill Literary House for being my home and community, and for helping me grow as a writer, editor, and literary citizen.

All of my love to my parents—Dana & Jay and Mark & Tina—who have always encouraged and pushed me. Love and gratitude to my brothers, Brett and Lyle, who have always challenged me and lifted me up. To my grandmothers, Jean and Patti, more gratitude and more love. To my Marky, everything and always.